BGK1027   Our God Reigns Piano Duets   arr. Nielson/Young

$14.95

Nielson & Young

Our God Reigns

Piano Duets by Stephen Nielson and Ovid Young

 Nielson &️ Young

 Red Rock Music Company

FOREWORD

Few would doubt that, of all man-made musical instruments, the piano best lends itself to solo playing. One pianist with only ten fingers can, by activating the eighty-eight keys which are fixed in a four-foot manual, produce melody, accompaniment, rhythm, counterpoint, atmospheric effects and background music, and all of this simultaneously!

The potential of the instrument is so great that pianists and composers very soon find themselves tempted to add more hands and fingers, just to realize even *more* of those wondrous possibilities.

Enter Nielson & Young. From the outset of our duo-piano collaboration more than three decades ago, we regularly created new works for two pianos/four hands, and commissioned others to contribute their unique compositional voices in an effort to enrich the duo-piano repertoire available to concert artists, young piano students and hard-working church musicians. The published music for this almost orchestral-sounding keyboard combination has grown quite large and richly diverse. A brand new setting of the classic Praise and Worship song, "Our God Reigns," enhances the familiar collection of hymntunes, old and new, which appear in this Nielson & Young artistic partnership with the Fred Bock Music Company.

The volume you hold in your hands contains duo-piano arrangements of familiar and beloved tunes whose origins span the 18th, 19th, 20th and 21st centuries. We hope you will lavish care and diligent practice on your preparation of these musical offerings. Your confident presentation of these settings will inspire the concert audiences and worshiping congregations for whom you perform them. *Soli Deo Gloria.*

Stephen Nielson and Ovid Young, *Duo-Pianists*

Nielson & Young are *Steinway* artists.

www.nielsonandyoung.com

Table of Contents

OUR GOD REIGNS

LEONARD E. SMITH, JR.
Arranged by NIELSON & YOUNG

JOYFUL, JOYFUL, WE ADORE THEE

("Hymn to Joy" from Beethoven's Ninth Symphony)

LUDWIG VAN BEETHOVEN
Arranged by NIELSEN & YOUNG

HOLY, HOLY, HOLY
(Nicea)

JOHN B. DYKES
Arranged by NIELSEN & YOUNG

ALL HAIL THE POWER
(Coronation)

Edward Perronet
John Rippon, alt.

OLIVER HOLDEN
Arranged by NIELSEN & YOUNG

HYMNS OF GOD AND COUNTRY

(Eternal Father, Strong to Save/God of Our Fathers)

Arranged by NIELSON & YOUNG

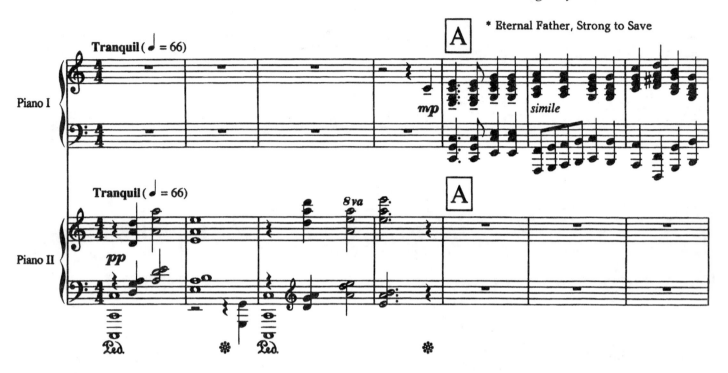

* God of Our Fathers

O THE DEEP, DEEP LOVE OF JESUS

(Ebenezer)

THOMAS J. WILLIAMS
Arranged by NIELSEN & YOUNG

When **Stephen Nielson** concluded his first full-length recital at age ten, many predicted what has become a stellar worldwide career. From his orchestral debut at eleven to success in international competitions to earning Distinguished Performer and Phi Beta Kappa honors at Indiana University's School of Music, he has certainly fulfilled that early promise.

His concertizing has taken him to such cities as Hong Kong, Bogota, Caracas, Freiburg, Copenhagen, Berlin, London, Vienna, Brussels, Tokyo, Dresden, Frankfurt, Prague, Salzburg, and Manchester. In addition, he has toured major artistic centers in Russia, the Baltics, Japan, and Switzerland, and has been chosen an official Ambassador of Culture by the World Cultural Alliance. His North American itinerary has taken him to such diverse locales as Los Angeles, Kansas City, Boston, Charlotte, Naples, Houston, Chicago, Miami, Detroit, Denver, Seattle, Dallas, Winnipeg, Toronto, Guadalajara, and Mexico City. Additionally, he has been active for many years as a chamber musician, having appeared across North America and Europe with some of the noteworthy violinists and cellists of our time.

Acclaiming his performance in Germany, the Berlin Morgenpost said, "Highly sensitive… articulate artistry," while Brussels' Le Soir reported that his was "exciting and masterful playing."

His discography includes recordings of the classical solo repertoire, music for piano and cello in collaboration with the celebrated cellist Anne Martindale Williams, and hymn tunes in the classical style. His writing achievements are listed in the catalogues of several American publishers. He enthusiastically maintains a limited teaching schedule for gifted young people and adults and conducts master classes in performance, practicing, and repertoire on a limited basis.

Since 1971, Mr. Nielson has been acclaimed for his role in the partnership of Nielson & Young, among the most active duo-piano teams on the musical scene today. Stephen Nielson and Ovid Young claim a breadth of repertoire and performance venues virtually without comparison, ranging from Oberammergau's Passion Play Theatre and various cruise ships to London's Royal Philharmonic Orchestra and Nashville's Grand Ole Opry House. The annual International Church Music Festival has taken Nielson & Young to Coventry, England and Bern, Switzerland, several times since 1985. Additional concertizing includes numerous venues in such cities as San Jose, Indianapolis, Calgary, Moscow, Vienna, Munich, Paris, and India.

Stephen Nielson and his wife, Carolyne, reside in Dallas and are the proud parents of two daughters, Christiana and Caroline, both promising young pianists in their own right.

One of the most versatile musicians before the concert public today, **Ovid Young** — pianist, organist, composer and conductor — has performed in major cities through the U.S.A. as well as in England, Germany, Austria, France, Switzerland, the Czech Republic, Japan, South Korea, Russia, Canada, Denmark, India, and the Caribbean. In his more than thirty year career, his mastery has been witnessed by hundreds of thousands of music lovers in a variety of concert settings.

Since 1971, Ovid Young has toured in partnership with fellow Texas pianist, Stephen Nielson, as the celebrated duo-piano team of Nielson & Young. They continue to log appearances in major concert halls, on university campuses, in churches, and in other venues as diverse as television studios and ocean-going cruise ships. Scheduled tours take them from coast-to-coast annually in the U.S. as well as to various locales in Europe and Asia. Nielson & Young began their long and distinguished concert career when both were serving on the music faculty of Olivet Nazarene University near Chicago.

As an organist, Dr. Young has played many of the largest and most interesting organs in America. This list includes the instruments at southern California's Crystal Cathedral, the Meyerson Symphony Center in Dallas, the Coral Ridge Presbyterian Church of Fort Lauderdale, the U. S. Air Force Academy Chapel, and the famous Wanamaker Grand Court organ in Philadelphia, as well as numerous cathedral and church organs in Europe.

In addition to his ongoing work with recording orchestras in the studios of Hollywood, New York, London, Nashville, Chicago, and Dallas, Ovid Young's performances with orchestras include the English Chamber Orchestra, the English Symphony, the Seoul (Korea) Philharmonic, the Bohuslav Martinu (Czech Republic) Philharmonic, the Danish Radio Symphony Orchestra, the Aarhus (Denmark) Symphony, the Florida Philharmonic, and the symphonies of Pittsburgh, Denver, Phoenix, and Nashville.

His many compositions and arrangements are offered by several American publishers. Recent commissioned works include an extended piece for the Texas All-State High School Orchestra, and music for five pianos/ten hands with symphony orchestra to be performed in a new show at Tokyo Disneyland. A composer of orchestral scores for several feature-length films, he is also widely remembered as the pianist-arranger-conductor for the renowned operatic singing duo of Robert Hale and Dean Wilder. Touring with Hale and Wilder for two decades across three continents produced fifteen albums of recorded music and scores of personal appearances on stage and television.

Ovid and his wife, Laura, are the parents of sons, Kirk and Erik, and reside in Dallas, Texas.

From the Press—

"Tivoli's Concert Hall was filled to the brim and the program consisted of nothing but hits, arranged and orchestrated by the solo pianist of the evening—Ovid Young. You needed only to sit back and enjoy the servings." *The Copenhagen Politiken (with the Danish Radio Symphony)*

"Ovid Young brought polished, delicately-sensitive playing to the Chopin and Schumann portions of the recital" *The Nashville Tennessean*

CREATIVE KEYBOARD COLLECTIONS

Piano and Organ Duets by Fred Bock

BOCK TO BOCK #1 . . . . BG0621   HL08738411
From a wonderful series of five volumes, this first collection features ten hymns specifically arranged for piano-organ duets. Titles include *And Can It Be, Love Was When, Moment By Moment, Near The Cross*, and more. Two copies are needed for performance. $10.95

BOCK TO BOCK #2 . . . . BG0686   HL08738412
The second volume of gospel greats for piano-organ duets features *My Tribute, Day By Day, Through It All, Ivory Palaces, Thou Art Worthy* and more. Two copies are needed for performance. $10.95

BOCK TO BOCK #3 . . . . BG0793   HL08738414
Fred Bock has again done a brilliant job arranging some of the most powerful contemporary Christian songs of today for piano-organ duets. Titles include *I've Just Seen Jesus, Great Is The Lord, How Majestic Is Your Name, In This Very Room, Majesty* and others. Two copies are needed for performance. $10.95

BOCK TO BOCK #4 *FOR CHRISTMAS* BG0821   HL08738415
Wonderful arrangements of several traditional and best-loved carols are housed in this collection for Christmas piano-organ duets, including *Away In a Manger, Joy To The World, There's a Song In the Air, Silent Night*, and others. Two copies are needed for performance. $10.95

BOCK TO BOCK #5 . . . . BG0909   HL08738417
Fred Bock concluded his organ and piano duet series with a fine cross-section of traditional hymnody and contemporary gospel songs. Titles include *Because He Lives, The Lord's Prayer, Lift High the Cross, Only Believe, Give Thanks, God of Grace and God of Glory* and more. Two copies are needed for performance. $10.95

SUNDAY MORNING WORSHIP BG0852   HL08738416
A collection of piano-organ duets, in the stylistic bravado of Fred Bock, includes majestic hymns *(Crown Him With Many Crowns, And Can It Be?, Joyful, Joyful We Adore Thee*, among others) as well as a popular Christmas title, *Angels We Have Heard on High*. Usable for the entire year. Two copies are needed for performance. $10.95

Organ and Piano Praise & Worship by Fred Bock

You asked for it, you got it! In Fred Bock's inimitable style of rich, lush harmonies, exciting rhythms, and tasty melodic intertwining, favorite praise and worship choruses are set in challenging and meaty arrangements for the experienced pianist and organist.

ORGAN-PIANO DUETS PRAISE AND WORSHIP *MEDLEYS* BG0757   HL08738413
An organ-piano duet collection of medleys of favorite praise songs, familiar hymns and gospel melodies. Four medleys of "Glorious, Majestic, Triumphant and Resplendent Praise" include *His Name Is Wonderful, He Is Exalted, To God Be The Glory, O For A Thousand Tongues To Sing, Holy, Holy, Holy* and many more. Two copies are needed for performance. $10.95

ORGAN PRAISE AND WORSHIP BG0923   HL08738404
Seven of the most popular of all praise and worship songs made entirely new by Fred Bock in this collection for organ. These are not typical hymn or gospel song settings; every one is a through-composed piece of music based on a praise and worship tune. Selections include *He Is Exalted, In My Life, Lord Be Glorified, We Will Glorify* and more. As Fred would say of this collection, *"This book will save your job!"* $10.95

See previous page for a listing of Praise & Worship collections for Piano by Fred Bock.

Exclusively distributed by Hal Leonard Corporation
Available from your local music retailer